JOHN HARBISON

FIVE SONGS of EXPERIENCE

for
Four Soloists, Four-Part Chorus
of Mixed Voices, String Quartet,
and Percussion

Set to Poems by
WILLIAM BLAKE

Associated Music Publishers, Inc.

DISTRIBUTED BY
HAL•LEONARD®
CORPORATION
7777 W. BLUEMOUND RD. P.O. BOX 13819 MILWAUKEE, WI 53213

JOHN HARBISON

John Harbison was born in Orange, New Jersey, in 1938. He studied at Harvard College and Princeton University before joining the faculty of the Massachusetts Institute of Technology in 1969. He is the first permanent holder of the Class of 1949 Professorship at MIT. From 1982 to 1984, at the request of André Previn, he was composer-in-residence with the Pittsburgh Symphony Orchestra, and from 1985 to 1987 held the same position at the Los Angeles Philharmonic, continuing his association with Previn.

Harbison has received commissions from the Koussevitzky, Fromm, Naumburg, and Rockefeller Foundations, as well as from many performing organizations, including anniversary commissions for the Boston Symphony (100th), New Haven Symphony (90th), and San Francisco Symphony (75th). His music has been performed by such organizations as the Aspen and Berkshire festivals, the San Francisco Opera, the New Opera Company (England), the New York Philharmonic, and the Fires of London. Recordings of Harbison's music are available on Nonesuch, CRI, and New World.

Also active as a conductor, Harbison has been music director of the Cantata Singers (1969-73, 1980-82) and co-director of the music ensemble, Collage (from 1984). He has conducted many orchestral and chamber ensembles, including the San Francisco, Boston, and Pittsburgh Symphonies, Speculum Musicae, and the Boston Symphony Chamber Players. Many of his works have been given their premieres by Harbison's wife, the violinist Rose Mary Harbison.

Harbison's cantata, *The Flight into Egypt*, received the Pulitzer Prize for music in 1987.

Composer's Note

I had long contemplated setting some of Blake's short poems to music, but given their finality and completeness, and their intense private meaning to each reader, I maintained a healthy wariness. Through my experience conducting the Cantata Singers and Ensemble, particularly in Schütz's music, a choral approach to the poems suggested itself. I began to hear them as incantation, response, or litany, in many kinds of vocal combination.

The calls for regeneration and reconciliation in the poems required a welcome effort to get back to beginnings and to be as inclusive, as little time-bound, as possible. The apparent simplicity, transparency, and subdued rhetoric of the poems suggested the creation of apparently-simple rhythms and harmonies.

INSTRUMENTATION

Performance requires a string quartet and two percussionists. (This piano reduction omits some pitches and percussion lines, and is for rehearsal only.)

PERCUSSION I

2 Bongos
3 Cow-Bells
2 Gongs
Bass Drum
Snare Drum
Maracas
Wood Block
2 Suspended Cymbals

PERCUSSION II

2 Congas
3 Temple Blocks
Tom-Tom
High Bell
2 Handbells 
Squeeze Drum
Claves

In No. 5 (A Divine Image) four percussion instruments are played by chorus members. Primitive instruments are intended, but the following substitutions are possible:

for African marimba: an orchestral marimba with snare sticks
for (Bermuda) steel drum: a xylophone with metal beater
for Finger harp: two automobile springs

An American Indian finger harp or a crude African one with wood frame and buzzing resonators is preferable to the African concert instrument.

STAGE POSITIONS

In No. 1 the solo chorus (made up of the four soloists) should be widely separated from the tutti chorus and instrumentalists, and closer to the audience. In Nos. 2 and 3 the soloists are in the normal position. In No. 5 the solo chorus is again separated, on the opposite side from that used in No. 1, and further from the audience.

Commissioned by Emmanuel Church, Boston, Craig Smith, music director

Five Songs of Experience

For Four Soloists, Four-Part Chorus of Mixed Voices, String Quartet and Percussion

William Blake

John Harbison

1. Introduction

* In this movement Soloists are to be widely separated from the chorus.

** Parts available from the publisher.

Printed in U. S. A.

A
Solo Soprano
Hear the voice of the Bard!
Solo Alto
ture sees; Who present, past, and future sees;
Solo Tenor
p
Whose ears have heard The Ho-ly Word, Whose ears have heard
Chorus Soprano
of the Bard!
Alto
sees; Who pres-ent, past, and fu-ture sees;
Tenor
p
Whose ears have heard The Ho-ly Word, Whose ears have heard The Ho-ly Word
A
I
pp
II

Solo Soprano
Hear the voice of the Bard!
Solo Tenor
The Ho - ly ___ Word,
Solo Bass
p
That walk'd ___ a-mong ___ the an - - cient trees, ___
Soprano
Hear the voice of the Bard!
Alto
Who pres - ent,
Chorus
Tenor
Whose ears have heard The Ho - ly Word, ___
Bass
p
That ___ walk'd a - mong the an - cient ___ trees,
I
p
Perc.
p stacc.
II

Solo Soprano
Hear the voice of the Bard! Hear
Solo Alto
Who pres - ent, past, and fu - ture sees;
Solo Tenor
Whose ears have heard The Ho - ly Word,
Solo Bass
That walk'd a - mong the
Soprano
Hear the voice of the Bard! Hear the
Chorus
Alto
past, and fu - ture sees; Who pres - ent, past, and fu - ture sees;
Tenor
Whose ears have heard The Ho - ly Word,
Bass
That walk'd a - mong the an - cient trees,
I
II

B
Solo Soprano
pp
— the voice of the Bard! —
Call - - - ing the lapsed soul, —
Solo Alto
Call - - - ing the lapsed soul, —
Solo Tenor
Call - - - ing the lapsed soul, —
Solo Bass
an - cient — trees,
Call - - - ing
Chorus Soprano
voice of the Bard!
Call - - - ing the
Alto
Call - - - ing the
Tenor
Call - - - ing the
Bass
That walk'd — a - mong — the an - - cient trees, —
Call - - - ing the
I
II

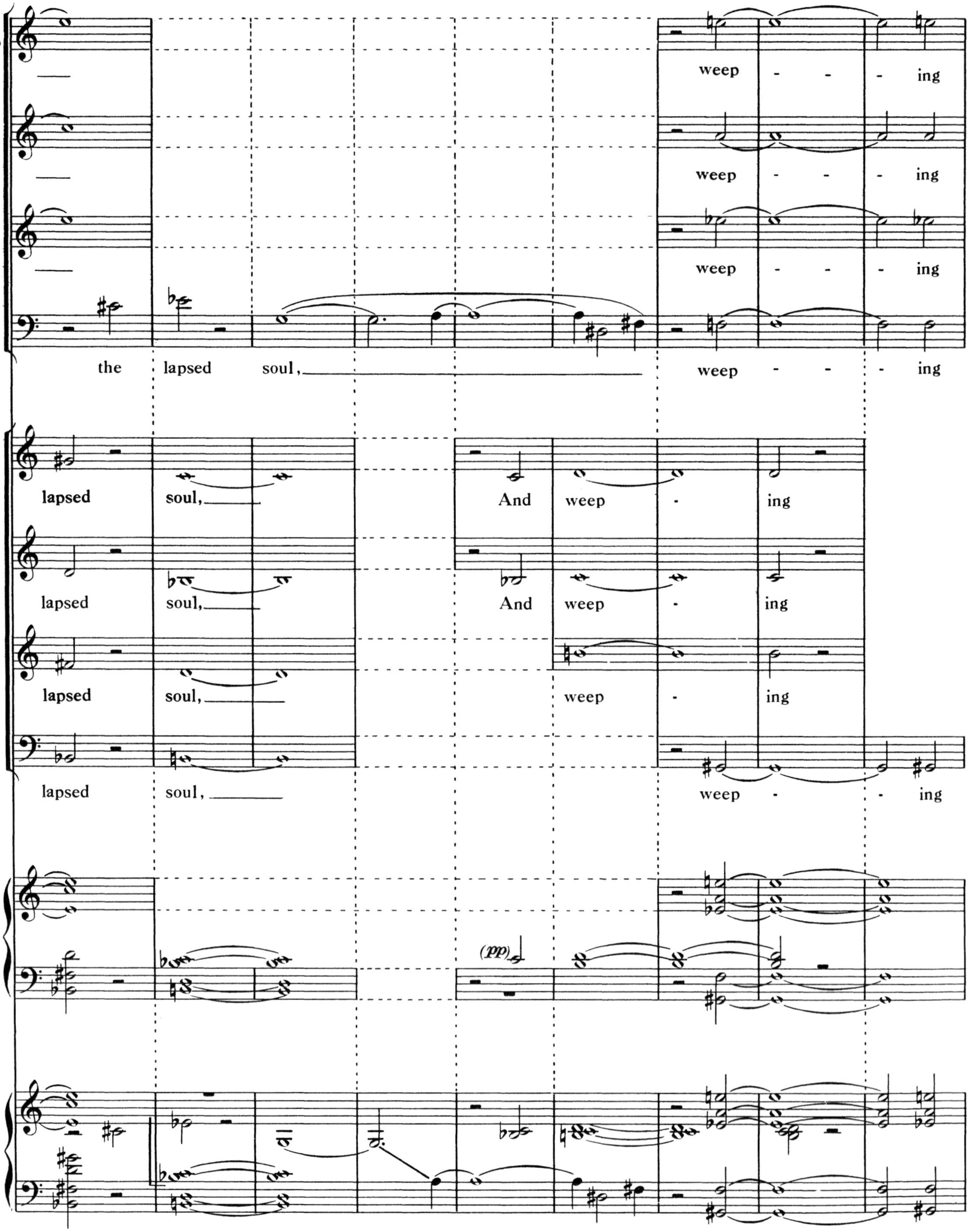
Solo Soprano
Solo Alto
Solo Tenor
Solo Bass
the lapsed soul, weep - - - ing
weep - - - ing
Chorus Soprano
Alto
Tenor
Bass
lapsed soul, And weep - ing
lapsed soul, weep - ing
lapsed soul, weep - - ing
(pp)
I
II

C
Solo Soprano
in the eve-ning dew;
Solo Alto
in the eve-ning dew;
Solo Tenor
in the eve-ning dew;
Solo Bass
in the eve-ning dew;
Chorus
Soprano
mp
That might con-trol
Alto
mp
That might con-trol
Bass
mp
That might con-trol The
Tenor
mp
That might con-trol The star-ry
C
I
mp
II

Solo
Solo Soprano
fall - en, fall - en, fall - en
Solo Alto
fall - en, fall - en, fall - en
Solo Tenor
fall - en, fall - en, fall - en
Solo Bass
fall - en, fall - en, fall - en
Chorus Soprano
The star - ry pole, And fall - en, fall - en light
Alto
The star - ry pole, And fall - en, fall - en light
Tenor
star-ry pole, And fall - en, fall - en light
Bass
pole, And fall - en, fall - en light
p
mp
cresc.
I
II

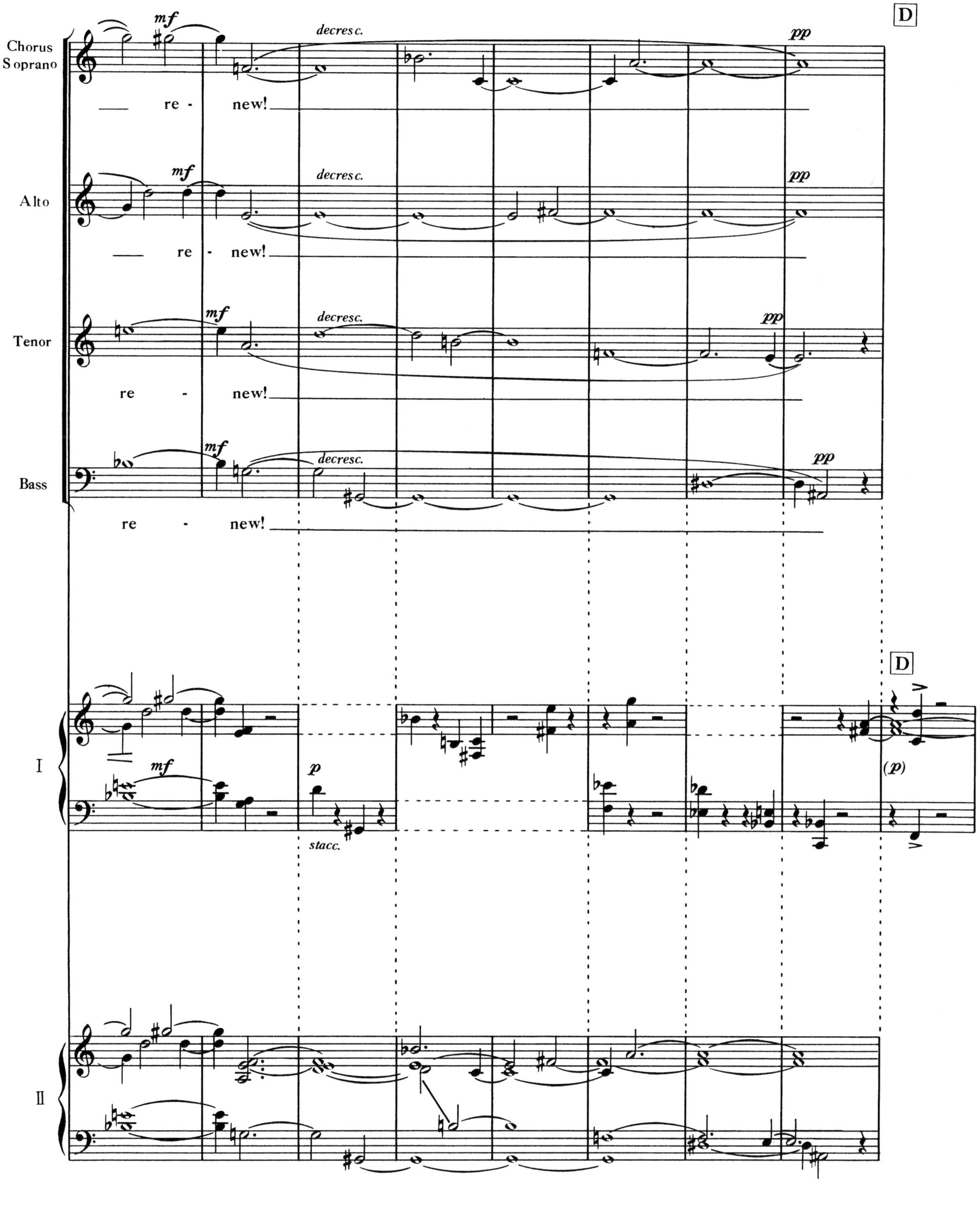
D
Chorus
Soprano
mf
decresc.
pp
re - new!
Alto
Tenor
Bass
stacc.
(p)
I
II

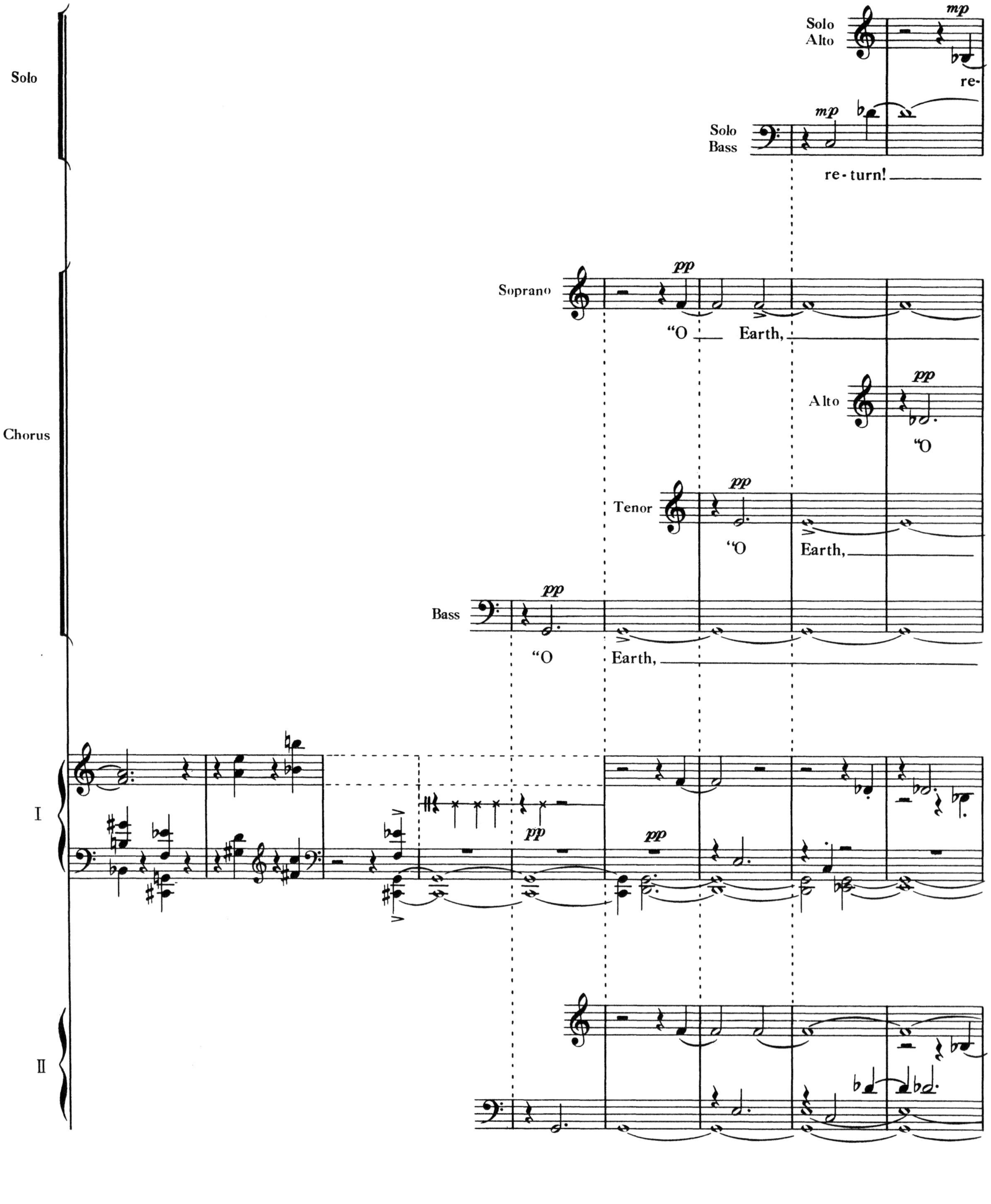
Solo
Chorus
I
II
Solo Alto
mp
re-
Solo Bass
mp
re-turn!
Soprano
pp
"O Earth,
Alto
pp
"O
Tenor
pp
"O
Earth,
Bass
pp
"O
Earth,
pp
pp

Solo Soprano
re - turn!
Solo Alto
turn!
A - rise from out
Solo Tenor
mp
A rise from out the dew - y grass;
Solo Bass
re - turn!
Chorus Soprano
O Earth!
O Earth!
Alto
Earth,
O Earth!
O Earth!
Tenor
O Earth!
Earth!
Bass
O Earth!
Earth!
I
II

E
Solo Soprano
A - rise from out the dew - y grass; Night is worn,
Solo Alto
the dew - y grass; Night is worn,
Solo Tenor
Night is
Solo Bass
Night is worn,
Chorus Soprano
Earth!
Alto
Earth!
Tenor
Earth!
Bass
Earth!
E
I
II

Solo Soprano
And the morn
Solo Alto
And the morn
mp
Solo Tenor
worn,
mp
Ris - es
Solo Bass
mp
Ris - - - - - - - - -
Chorus Soprano
p
Night is worn,
Alto
p
Night is worn,
mp
from
Tenor
p
Night is worn,
Bass
p
Night is worn,
mp
from
I
p
mp
II

Solo Soprano
mp mf
slum - - berous
Solo Alto
mf
slum - berous
Solo Tenor
mf decresc.
slum - berous
Solo Bass
es
Chorus
Soprano
mp mf decresc. mp
mass.
Alto
mf decresc. mp
the
mass.
Tenor
mp mf decresc. mp
from the
mass.
Bass
the
mf
I
II

F
Solo Soprano
Why wilt thou turn a-way?
Solo Alto
Why wilt thou turn a-way?
Solo Tenor
Turn a - way no more;
Solo Bass
Turn a - way no more;
Chorus Soprano
decresc.
Why wilt thou turn a-way?
Alto
decresc.
Why wilt thou turn a-way?
Tenor
Turn a - way no more; Turn a - way no more; Turn
Bass
Turn a - way no more; Turn a - way no more; Turn
F
stacc.
I
II

Solo Soprano
Why wilt thou turn a-way? Why
Solo Alto
Why wilt thou turn a-way? Why
Solo Tenor
Turn a - way no more; Turn a - way no more;
Solo Bass
Turn a - way no more; Turn a - way no more;
Soprano
Why wilt thou turn a-way? Why wilt
Alto
Why wilt thou turn a-way? Why wilt
Chorus Tenor
a - way no more; Turn a - way no more;
Bass
a - way no more; Turn a - way no more;
I
II

G
Solo Soprano
wilt thou turn a-way? The star - ry floor, The wa - t'ry
Solo Alto
wilt thou turn a-way? The star - ry floor, The wa - t'ry
Solo Tenor
The star - ry floor, The wa - t'ry
Solo Bass
The star - ry floor, The wa - t'ry
Chorus Soprano
thou turn a-way? The star - ry floor, The wa - t'ry shore,
Alto
thou turn a-way? The star - ry floor, The wa - t'ry shore,
Tenor
The star - ry floor, The wa - t'ry shore,
Bass
The star - ry floor, The wa - t'ry shore,
G
I
f sost.
II

Solo Soprano
Solo Alto
Solo Tenor
Solo Bass
decresc.
mf
shore, Is giv'n thee till the break of day, of
Chorus Soprano
Alto
Tenor
Bass
decresc.
mf
mp
Is giv'n thee till the break of day, of day,
I
II

Solo Soprano
day,
day,
day."
Solo Alto
day,
day,
day."
Solo Tenor
day,
day,
day."
Solo Bass
day,
day,
day."
Chorus Soprano
day."
Alto
day."
Tenor
day."
Bass
day."
I
II

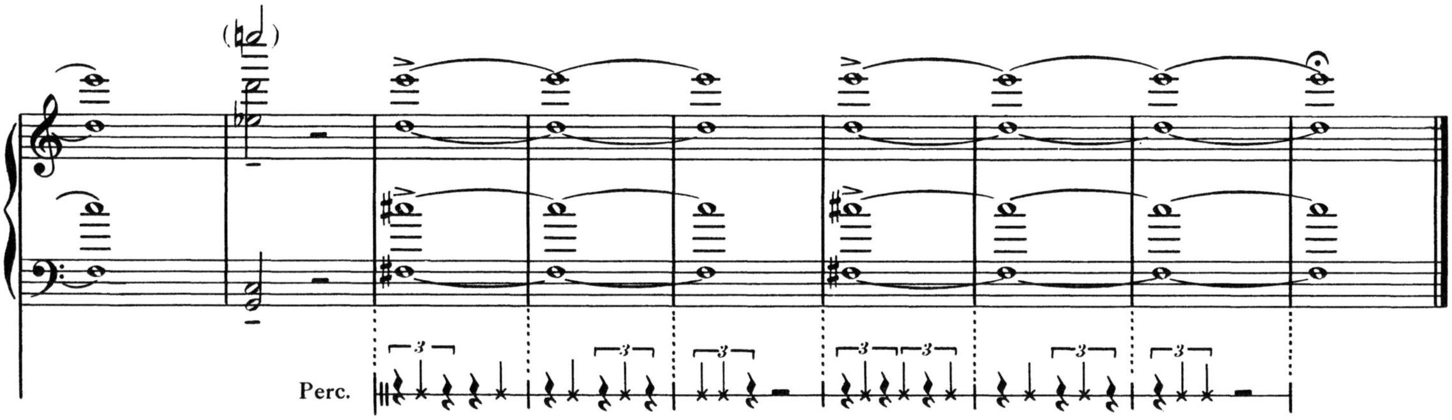

2. Earth's Answer

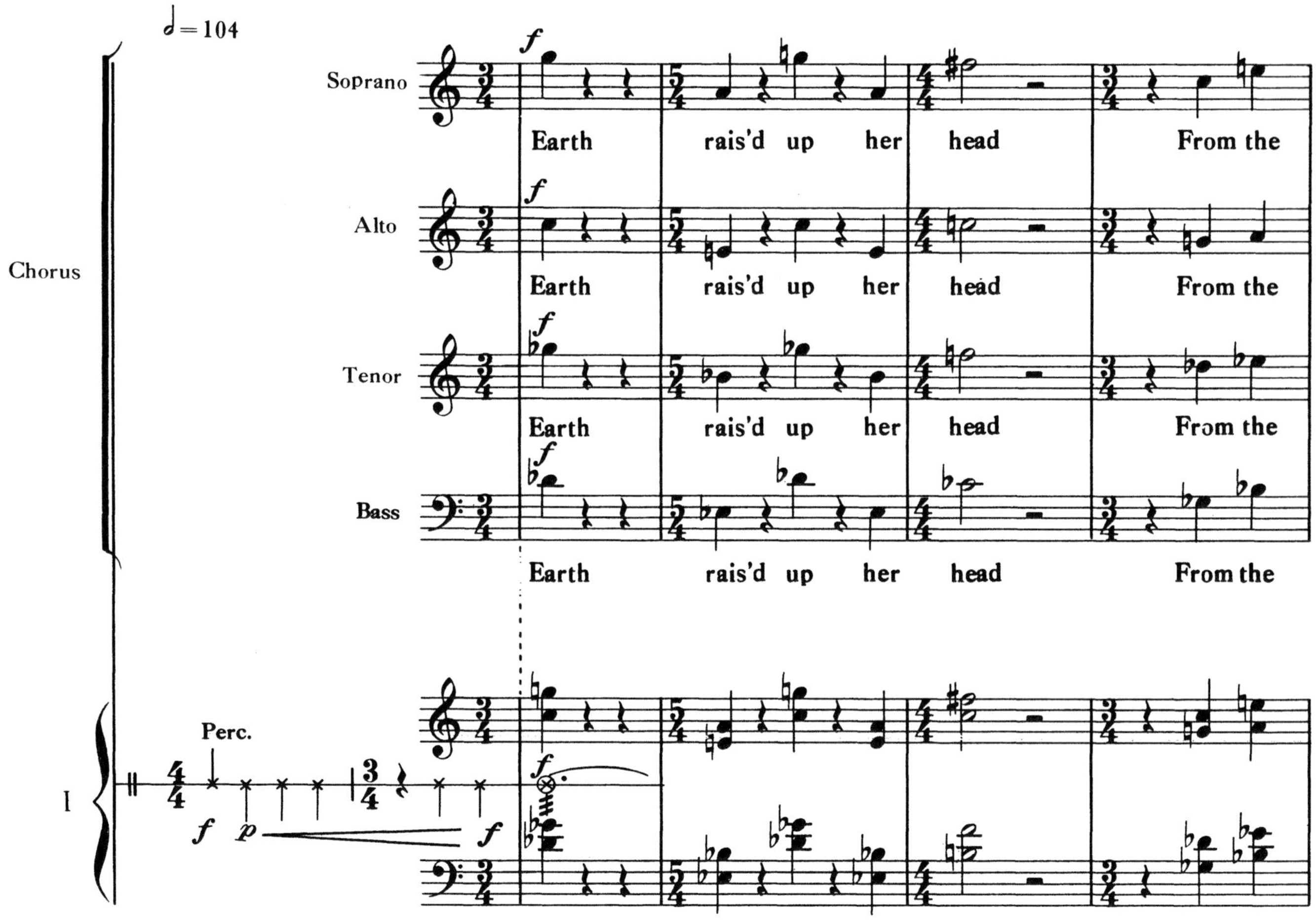

Chorus Soprano
Alto
Tenor
Bass
I
dark-ness dread and drear. Her light fled, Sto - ny
dread! And her locks cov-er'd with grey de - spair.
Tenor Solo
"Pris - oned
f

Solo Tenor
Chorus
I
H
on wa - t'ry shore, Star-ry Jeal - ous - y
mf (whispered)
Tutti
Earth rais'd up her head
sempre f
does keep my den; Cold and hoar,
weep - - - - - - - - - - ing o'er, I hear

I
Solo Tenor
the fa - ther of the an - cient men.
Chorus
Tutti
From the
sempre f
Bass
Self - ish fa - ther of men!
Chorus Tutti
dark-ness dread and drear.
Solo Bass
Cru-el, jeal - ous, self - ish fear! Can

Solo Bass
de - light,
Chain'd
J
Solo Alto
Does
in night,
The vir - gins of
youth and morn -
(f)
I
spring
hide its joy
- ing bear?
Chorus Tutti
Her locks

Solo Alto
When buds and blos - soms grow? Does the
Chorus
cov er'd with grey de - spair,
I
sow - er Sow by night. Or the plow -
K
(f)
man in dark - ness plow?
Her light fled, Sto - ny

Solo Alto
'Break this heav - - - - - - - - y chain That does
Solo Tenor
'Break this heav - - - - y chain That does
Bass
'Break
Solo Bass
this heav - y chain That does
Chorus Tutti
dread!
I
II

L
Solo Alto
freeze my bones a - round.
Self-ish!
Solo Tenor
freeze my bones a - round.
Self-ish!
Solo Bass
freeze my bones a - round.
Self-ish!
Chorus Soprano
Earth rais'd up her head From the dark-ness dread and drear.
Alto
Earth rais'd up her head From the dark-ness dread and drear.
Tenor
Earth rais'd up her head From the dark-ness dread and drear.
Bass
Earth rais'd up her head From the dark-ness dread and drear.
L
I
più f
II
High bell trill

Solo Alto
vain! E - ter - nal bane! That
Solo Tenor
vain! E - ter - nal bane! That
Solo Bass
vain! E - ter - nal bane! That
Chorus Soprano
Her light fled, Ston - y dread! And her locks cov-er'd with grey
Alto
Her light fled, Ston - y dread! And her locks cov-er'd with grey
Tenor
Her light fled, Ston - y dread! And her locks cov-er'd with grey
Bass
Her light fled, Ston - y dread! And her locks cov-er'd with grey
I
II

Solo Alto
free
Love
with
bon
-
dage
Solo Tenor
free
Love
with
bon
-
-
Solo Bass
free - - - - -
Love
with
Chorus Soprano
de - spair.
Alto
de - spair.
Tenor
de - spair.
Bass
de - spair.
I
II

Solo Alto
bound.'"
Solo Tenor
– dage bound'."
Solo Bass
— bon - - - - - - dage bound.'"
II
M
f
sim.
I
I

3. Ah! Sun-Flower

Solo Soprano
I
Where the
Tempo II
rit.
Tempo I
Youth pined a-way with de-sire, And the pale Vir-gin shroud-ed in snow,
accel.
Tempo II
A-rise from their graves, and as-pire

rit.
Tempo I
decresc.
Solo Soprano
Where my Sun - flow-er wish-es to go.
I
O
Chorus
Soprano
Alto
Tenor
Bass
Ah, Sun - flow-er! Ah,
Ah, Sun - flow-er! Ah, Sun - flow-er!

Tempo II
Solo Soprano
Sun-flow-er! wea - - - - - - - - - - - - - - - ry of time, Who
Chorus Soprano
wea - - - - - - - - - - - - - - ry,
Alto
wea - - - - - - - - - - - - - ry,
Tenor
wea - ry, wea - ry, wea - ry,
Bass
wea - ry, wea - ry, wea - ry,
Tempo II
I
rit. Tempo I
count est the steps of the Sun, Seek - ing
decresc.
Soprano
Seek - - - - - - - - ing
Alto
Seek - - - - - - - - ing
Tenor
Seek - - - - - - - -
Bass
Seek - - - - - -
Chorus
rit. Tempo I
I

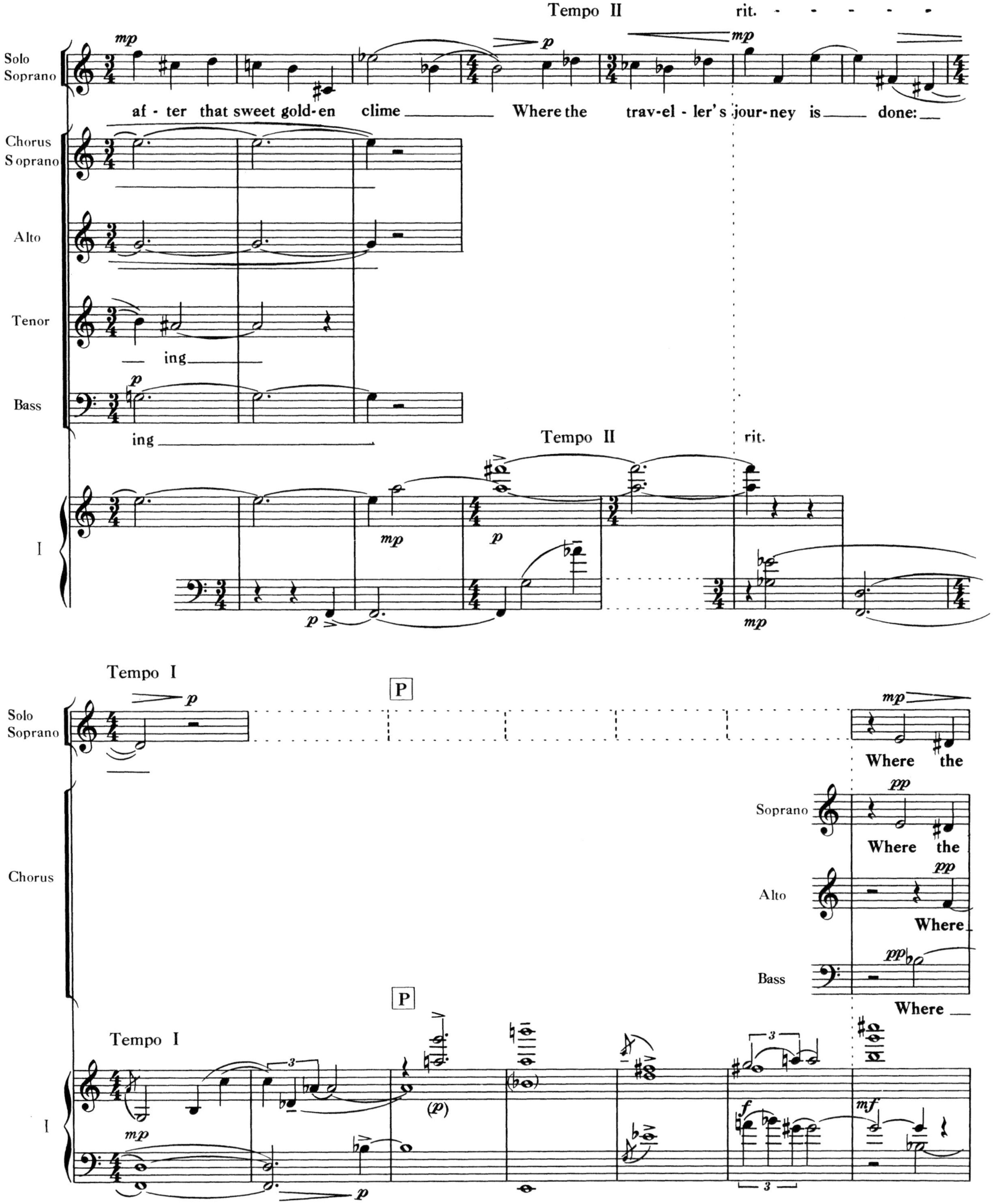
Tempo II
rit.
Solo Soprano
af - ter that sweet gold - en clime Where the trav - el - ler's jour - ney is done:
Chorus Soprano
Alto
Tenor
ing
Bass
ing
Tempo II
rit.
I
Tempo I
P
Solo Soprano
Where the
Chorus
Soprano
Where the
Alto
Where
Bass
Where
P
Tempo I
I

Solo Soprano
Chorus Soprano
Alto
Tenor
Bass
I
Tempo II
rit.
Youth pined a-way with de-sire, And the
Youth
the Youth
And the
Tempo I
pale Vir-gin Shroud-ed in snow,
decresc.
pale Vir-gin
A-rise
Q

accel.
Tempo II
Solo Soprano
Chorus Soprano
Alto
Tenor
Bass
A - rise
from their graves,
and as -
pire
Ah
Where my Sun - - - - - - flow - er
and as - pire
Where my Sun - flow - er
I

R
Solo Soprano
Chorus Soprano
wish-es to go.
wish-es to go.
Alto
Where my Sun - flow-er wish es to go.
Tenor
wish - es to go.
Bass
wish - es to go.
R
I
Solo Soprano
Chorus Soprano
Alto
I
f

4. The Voice of the Ancient Bard

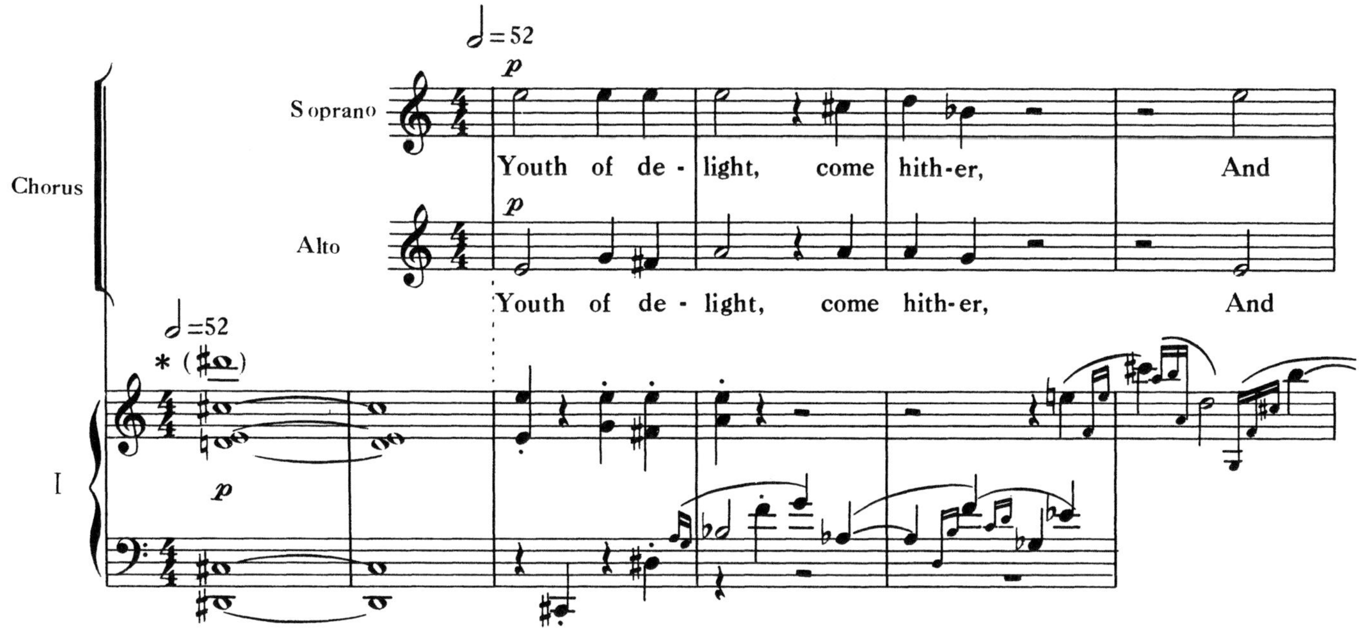

* In this movement many doublings of vocal lines are not included in the instrumental reduction.

Chorus Soprano
new born. Doubt is fled, and clouds of rea-son,
Alto
new born. Doubt is fled, and clouds of rea-son,
I
stacc.
Chorus Soprano
mp
Dark dis-putes and art-ful teas-ing,
Alto
mp
Dark dis-putes and art-ful teas-ing,
I
mp
p
p
S
Chorus Tenor
p
Fol-ly is an end-less maze, Tan - gled roots perplex her ways.
Bass
p
Fol-ly is an end-less maze, Tan - gled roots per-plex her ways.
S
I
p
mp
p

Chorus Tenor
How man - - - - - y have fall- en there! They stum- ble
Bass
How man - - - - - y have fall- en there! They stum- ble
I
mp
Chorus Tenor
all night o- ver bones of the dead, And feel they know not what but care,
Bass
all night o- ver bones of the dead, And feel they know not what but care,
p
Chorus Tenor
And wish to lead oth- ers when they should be led.
mp
Bass
And wish to lead oth- ers, when they should be led.
mp
I
mp
mp
mp

I
decresc.
p
T
Chorus Soprano
Youth of de - light, come hith- er, And see the
Alto
Youth of de - light, come hith-er, And see the
Tenor
Fol - ly is an end-less maze, Tan - gled roots per-plex her ways.
Bass
Fol - ly is an end-less maze, Tan - gled roots per-plex her ways.
T
I
II

Chorus
Soprano
Alto
Tenor
Bass
I
II
ope-ning morn,
Im-age of truth
ope-ning morn,
Im-age of truth
How man-y have fall-en there!
They stum-ble
How man-y have fall-en there!
They stum-ble

Chorus Soprano
new born. Doubt is fled, and clouds of
Alto
new born. Doubt is fled, and clouds of
Tenor
all night o-ver bones of the dead, And feel they know not what but care,
Bass
all night o-ver bones of the dead, And feel they know not what but care,
I
II

U
Chorus Soprano
rea-son, Dark dis-putes and art-ful teas-ing.
Alto
rea-son, Dark dis-putes and art-ful teas-ing.
Tenor
And wish to lead oth-ers when they should be led.
Bass
And wish to lead oth-ers when they should be led.
U
I
II
I
I

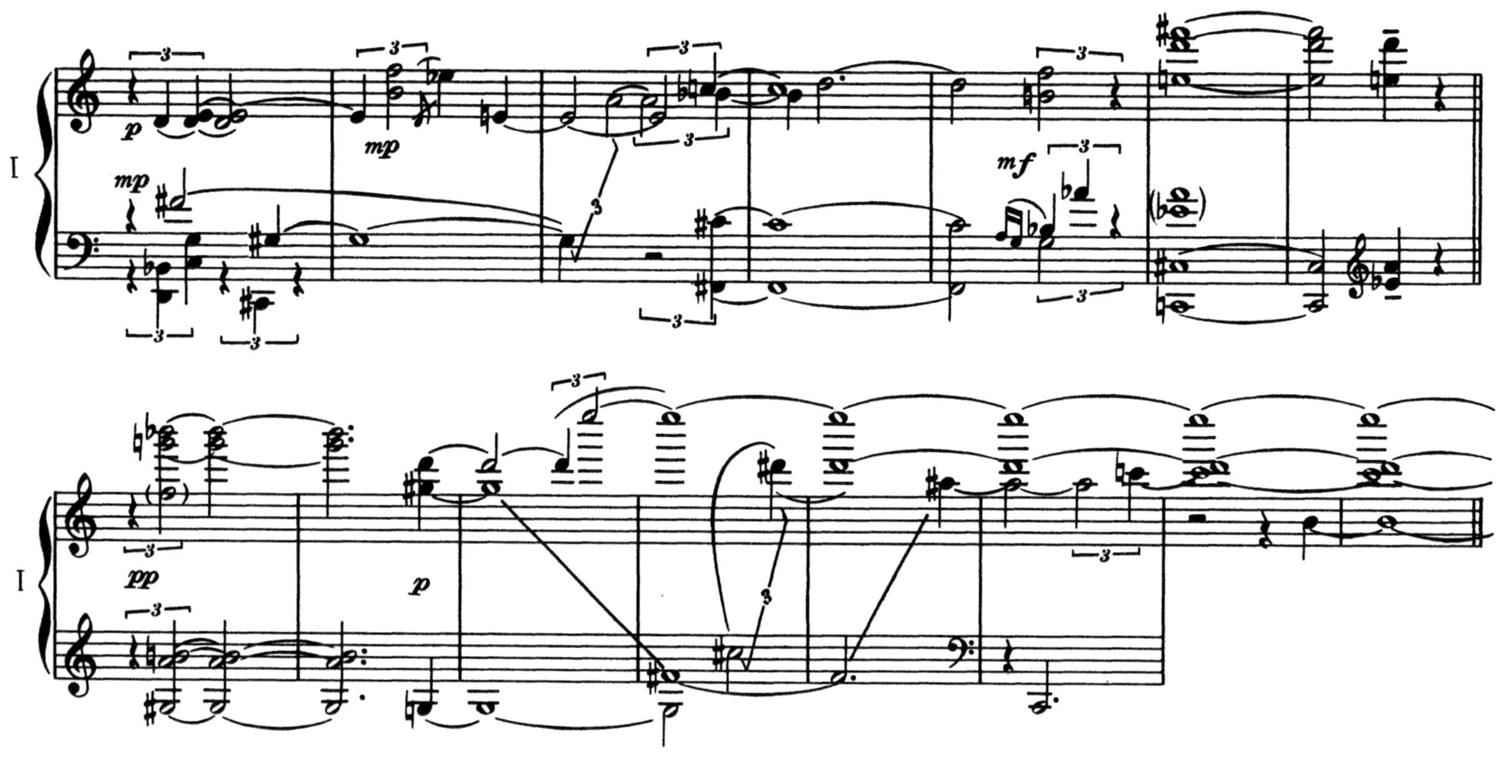

5. A Divine Image

* Played by a chorus member. Pitches may be indefinite, depending upon instruments used.

Chorus Tutti
Soprano
ff
(simile)
Cru-el - ty has a
Alto
ff
Cru-el - ty has a
Tenor
ff
Cru-el - ty has a
Bass
ff
Cru-el - ty has a
Chorus Perc.
(simile)
II

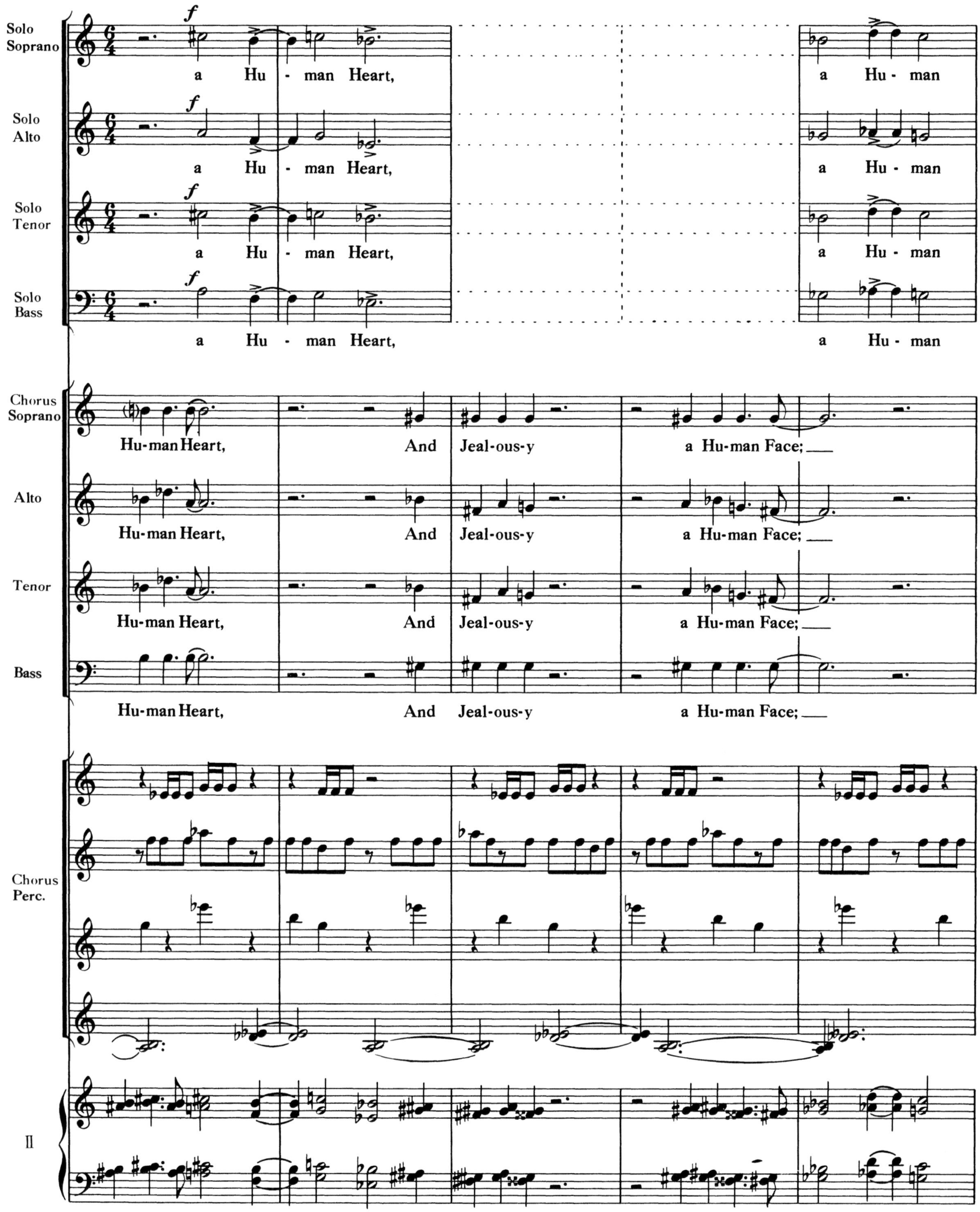
Solo Soprano
a Hu - man Heart,
a Hu - man
Solo Alto
a Hu - man Heart,
a Hu - man
Solo Tenor
a Hu - man Heart,
a Hu - man
Solo Bass
a Hu - man Heart,
a Hu - man
Chorus Soprano
Hu-man Heart, And Jeal-ous-y a Hu-man Face;
Alto
Hu-man Heart, And Jeal-ous-y a Hu-man Face;
Tenor
Hu-man Heart, And Jeal-ous-y a Hu-man Face;
Bass
Hu-man Heart, And Jeal-ous-y a Hu-man Face;
Chorus Perc.
II

Solo Soprano
Face; the Hu - man Form, the Hu -
Solo Alto
Face; the Hu - man Form, the Hu -
Solo Tenor
Face; the Hu - man Form, the Hu -
Solo Bass
Face; the Hu - man Form, the Hu -
Chorus Soprano
Ter-ror the Hu-man Form Di - vine, And Se-cre-cy the Hu-man Dress.
Alto
Ter-ror the Hu-man Form Di - vine, And Se-cre-cy the Hu-man Dress.
Tenor
Ter-ror the Hu-man Form Di - vine, And Se-cre-cy the Hu-man Dress.
Bass
Ter-ror the Hu-man Form Di - vine, And Se-cre-cy the Hu-man Dress.
Chorus Perc.
II

Solo Soprano
- man Dress.
Solo Alto
- man Dress.
Solo Tenor
- man Dress.
Solo Bass
- man Dress.
Chorus Perc.
Perc.
ff
II

V
Solo Soprano
The Hu - man Dress, The Hu - man Form,
Solo Alto
The Hu - man Dress, The Hu - man Form,
Solo Tenor
The Hu - man Dress, The Hu - man
Solo Bass
The Hu man Dress, The Hu - man
Chorus
Soprano
The Hu-man Dress is for-ged Iron,
Alto
The Hu-man Dress is for-ged Iron,
Tenor
The Hu-man Dress is for-ged Iron,
Bass
The Hu-man Dress is for-ged Iron,
V
Chorus Perc.
II

Solo Soprano
The Hu - man Face,
Solo Alto
The Hu - man Face,
Solo Tenor
Form,
The Hu - man Face,
Solo Bass
Form,
The Hu - man Face,
Chorus Soprano
The Hu-man Form a fie - ry Forge,
The Hu - man Face,
Alto
The Hu-man Form a fie - ry Forge,
The Hu - man Face,
Tenor
The Hu-man Form a fie - ry Forge,
The Hu - man Face,
Bass
The Hu-man Form a fie - ry Forge,
The Hu - man Face,
Chorus Perc.
II

Solo
Solo Soprano
The Hu - man Heart.
Solo Alto
The Hu - man Heart.
Solo Tenor
The Hu - man Heart.
Solo Bass
The Hu - man Heart.
Chorus Soprano
a Fur-nace seal'd, The Hu-man Heart its hun- gry
Alto
a Fur-nace seal'd, The Hu-man Heart its hun- gry
Tenor
a Fur-nace seal'd, The Hu-man Heart its hun- gry
Bass
a Fur-nace seal'd, the Hu-man Heart its hun- gry
II

W
Solo Soprano
Gorge.
Solo Alto
Gorge.
Solo Tenor
Gorge.
Solo Bass
Gorge.
W
Chorus Perc.
5
5
II

Chorus
Perc.
5
5
Chorus
Perc.